COOL CARS

MERCEDES

BY DALTON RAINS

WWW.APEXEDITIONS.COM

Copyright © 2026 by Apex Editions, Mendota Heights, MN 55120. All rights reserved. No part of this book may be reproduced or utilized in any form or by any means without written permission from the publisher.

Apex is distributed by North Star Editions:
sales@northstareditions.com | 888-417-0195

Produced for Apex by Red Line Editorial.

Photographs ©: Pixabay, cover; Shutterstock Images, 1, 10–11, 12, 13, 14–15, 16–17, 18, 19, 21, 22–23, 24–25, 26, 27, 29; Clive Mason/Getty Images Sport/Getty Images, 4–5, 6–7; Bryn Lennon/Getty Images Sport/Getty Images, 8–9

Library of Congress Control Number: 2025930274

ISBN
979-8-89250-525-3 (hardcover)
979-8-89250-561-1 (paperback)
979-8-89250-632-8 (ebook pdf)
979-8-89250-597-0 (hosted ebook)

Printed in the United States of America
Mankato, MN
082025

NOTE TO PARENTS AND EDUCATORS

Apex books are designed to build literacy skills in striving readers. Exciting, high-interest content attracts and holds readers' attention. The text is carefully leveled to allow students to achieve success quickly. Additional features, such as bolded glossary words for difficult terms, help build comprehension.

CHAPTER 1
COMEBACK FINISH 4

CHAPTER 2
HISTORY 10

CHAPTER 3
MAIN RANGE 16

CHAPTER 4
WILDEST CARS 22

COMPREHENSION QUESTIONS • 28
GLOSSARY • 30
TO LEARN MORE • 31
ABOUT THE AUTHOR • 31
INDEX • 32

CHAPTER 1

COMEBACK FINISH

The Turkish **Grand Prix** begins. It's one of the last races of the 2020 **Formula 1** season. Lewis Hamilton's Mercedes zooms along the track.

Lewis Hamilton races for Mercedes during the 2020 Turkish Grand Prix.

Hamilton starts off stuck in sixth place. But by lap 37, he is in second. He **drafts** behind the leader. Then, Hamilton's engine roars. He moves his Mercedes into first place.

Hamilton (44) leads a group of drivers during the Turkish Grand Prix.

RACE ON

Most cars took two **pit stops** during the Turkish Grand Prix. But Hamilton took only one pit stop. So did the leader at lap 37. They went ahead while others got repairs.

Hamilton crosses the finish line with a big lead. He wins his seventh Drivers' Championship.

FAST FACT

Between 2014 and 2021, Mercedes won eight Constructors' Championships. That title goes to the best racing team.

With his seventh title, Hamilton tied the record for most Drivers' Championships ever.

CHAPTER 2

History

Gottlieb Daimler and Carl Benz were **engineers**. In the 1880s, their companies built the first modern cars. The two men never met. But their companies joined in 1926.

In 1886, Gottlieb Daimler built the Daimler Motor Carriage.

The SSK helped Mercedes win many Grand Prix in the late 1920s and early 1930s.

The new company mostly made **luxury** cars. After World War II (1939–1945), Mercedes added more kinds of cars. It made vans and trucks, too.

RACING HISTORY

Mercedes joined Formula 1 in 1954. In 1955, one of its cars crashed and exploded. Car pieces flew into the crowd. More than 80 people died. Afterward, Mercedes left Formula 1. It started racing again in 2010.

Mercedes came out with the 300 SL in the 1950s. It featured gull-wing doors that swung up to open.

A limousine version of the Mercedes-Benz 600 became popular with the leaders of many countries.

Mercedes grew quickly. It became popular worldwide. One famous car was the Mercedes-Benz 600. It sold from 1963 to 1981.

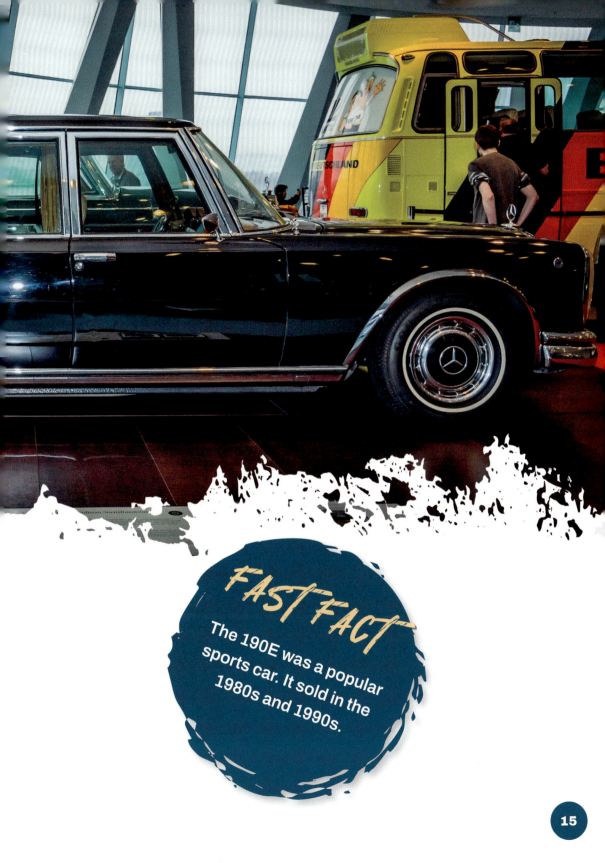

FAST FACT

The 190E was a popular sports car. It sold in the 1980s and 1990s.

CHAPTER 3

MAIN RANGE

By the 2020s, Mercedes sold many kinds of vehicles. The C-Class was popular and less expensive. The car came as a two-door coupe or a four-door sedan.

People could buy a convertible version of the Mercedes C-Class.

Mercedes made sure the insides of its cars were just as beautiful as the outsides.

Mercedes was most known for its S-Class series. These cars showed off the owners' wealth. One model even had massaging seats.

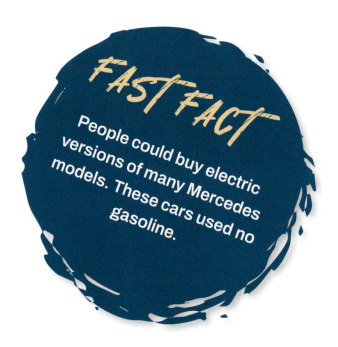

FAST FACT

People could buy electric versions of many Mercedes models. These cars used no gasoline.

The Mercedes-Maybach was one of the fanciest S-Class cars.

Mercedes also built a variety of SUVs. The GLC and GLE were two top sellers. All of Mercedes's SUVs showed off space, power, and luxury.

G-CLASS

The Mercedes G-Class combined style and utility. The SUV was made for off-road driving. Different driving settings let it travel over rock or sand.

The G-Class SUV was originally meant to be used in militaries.

CHAPTER 4

WILDEST CARS

Mercedes's **supercars** drew attention wherever they went. The AMG GT was light and powerful. It was good for long trips. But drivers could also take the sporty car to the track.

Mercedes showed off its first AMG GT in 2014. In 2023, Mercedes released the second version of the GT.

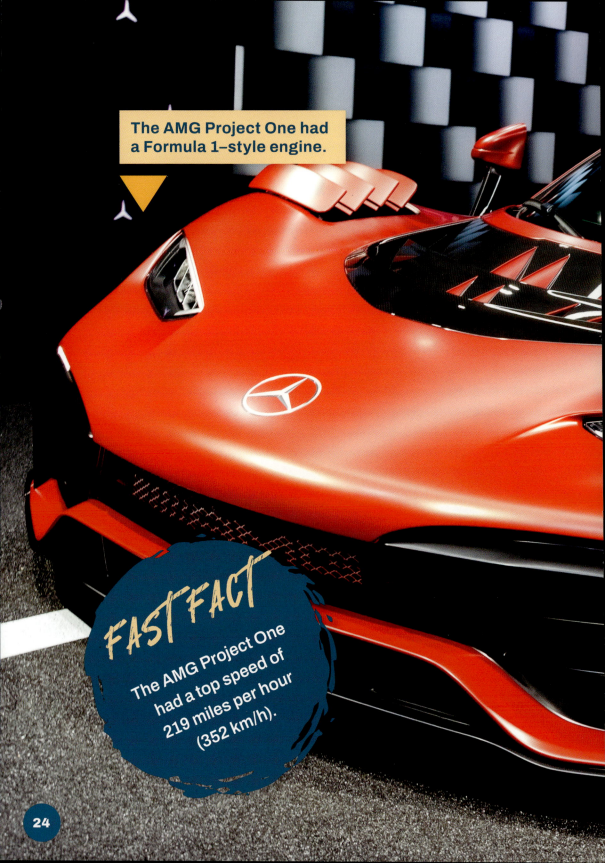

The AMG Project One had a Formula 1–style engine.

FAST FACT
The AMG Project One had a top speed of 219 miles per hour (352 km/h).

The AMG Project One was built like a race car. Large vents kept the engine cool. Flaps and fins kept the ride smooth.

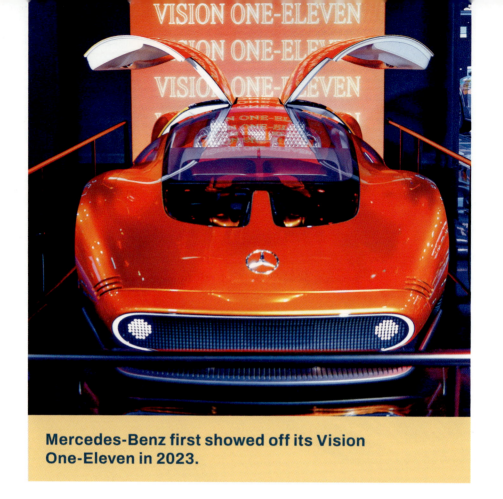

Mercedes-Benz first showed off its Vision One-Eleven in 2023.

Mercedes also built **concept cars**. The Vision One-Eleven had a flowing look and high-tech batteries. It made people excited to see what Mercedes would build next.

MOVIE MAGIC

The Vision AVTR had a striking look. Its design was based on the movie *Avatar*. Colorful lights and natural-looking curves made the car feel alive.

The wheels of the Vision AVTR could move sideways and diagonally.

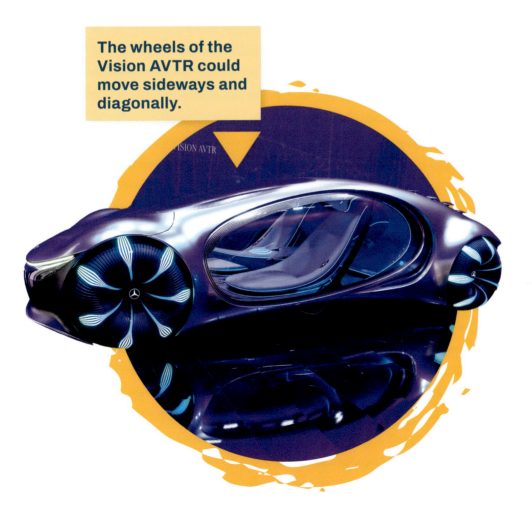

COMPREHENSION QUESTIONS

Write your answers on a separate piece of paper.

1. Write a few sentences explaining the main ideas of Chapter 2.

2. Which Mercedes model would you most like to have? Why?

3. Which Mercedes driver won the 2020 Turkish Grand Prix?
   - A. Lewis Hamilton
   - B. Gottlieb Daimler
   - C. Carl Benz

4. Which of these cars did Mercedes make first?
   - A. the 600
   - B. the 190E
   - C. the C-Class

5. What does **utility** mean in this book?

The Mercedes G-Class combined style and ***utility****. The SUV was made for off-road driving. Different driving settings let it travel over rock or sand.*

    A. features that look good
    B. useful features
    C. unhelpful features

6. What does **design** mean in this book?

The Vision AVTR had a striking look. Its ***design*** *was based on the movie* Avatar*. Colorful lights and natural-looking curves made the car feel alive.*

    A. the speed of something
    B. the cost of something
    C. the look of something

Answer key on page 32.

GLOSSARY

concept cars
Vehicles that show new technologies or designs.

drafts
Follows another race car very closely to travel faster.

engineers
People who use math and science to solve problems.

Formula 1
The highest level of open-wheel racing.

Grand Prix
A car race on a difficult course that is part of a world championship series.

luxury
Having to do with things that are high quality, comfortable, and often expensive.

pit stops
Times when race cars stop to get fuel or repairs.

supercars
Cars fast enough for racing that can also go on the street.

BOOKS

Duling, Kaitlyn. *Mercedes AMG GT*. Bellwether Media, 2024.

Maurer, Tracy Nelson. *S-Class by Mercedes-Benz*. Crabtree Publishing Company, 2022.

Rains, Dalton. *Formula 1 Racing*. Apex Editions, 2024.

ONLINE RESOURCES

Visit **www.apexeditions.com** to find links and resources related to this title.

ABOUT THE AUTHOR

Dalton Rains is a writer and editor from St. Paul, Minnesota. He would love to drive a Mercedes someday.

INDEX

#
190E, 15

A
AMG GT, 22
AMG Project One, 24–25

B
Benz, Carl, 10

C
C-Class, 16
Constructors' Championship, 8

D
Daimler, Gottlieb, 10
Drivers' Championship, 8

F
Formula 1, 4, 6–8, 13

G
G-Class, 20
GLC, 20
GLE, 20

H
Hamilton, Lewis, 4, 6–8

M
Mercedes-Benz 600, 14

S
S-Class, 18

T
Turkish Grand Prix, 4, 6–8

V
Vision AVTR, 27
Vision One-Eleven, 26

ANSWER KEY:
1. Answers will vary; 2. Answers will vary; 3. A; 4. A; 5. B; 6. C